Drawn C
an alphabet of birds
Dru Marland

Bristol

Gert Macky Books
mmxvii

first published in 2017 by
Gert Macky Books
4 Cotham Vale, Bristol, BS6 6HR
drusilla.marland@gmail.com
gertmacky.co.uk

printed by minutemanbristol.com

ISBN 978-0-9926783-3-3

to Katie, who is still pretty wild

I've written about and drawn birds I'm familiar with, if only
(in the case of the ptarmigan) in the pages of books. So they're all
birds you'll find in Britain, except for the albatross. But then I've
seen an albatross, and I've yet to see an avocet.

Acknowledgements

Thanks to all the friends who suggested tweaks and corrections;
to Deborah Harvey and Jinny Peberday for proofreading;
to Peter Hunter for his inspired suggestion of V for geese.
And Peter and Lucie at Minuteman Press in Bristol, for their
cheerful help and excellent printing.

The albatross, the albatross!
Of birds pelagic, it's the boss;
its wingspan is ten feet across
and sometimes even greater.

It scorns the tropics, rides the storm;
one moment here, the next one gorn
a thousand miles beyond Cape Horn,
but never the equator.

The sailor says it brings good luck;
if by an arrow it is struck
you can be sure your goose is cooked
and you'll be sorry later.

a distant jet plane
and a blackbird chipping chinks
from the dawn's silence

Cormorants always hark right back to
ancient rels the pterodactyls;
they say, "We once were huge – like this!"
and spread their wings for emphasis.
Still, they live mostly blameless lives,
though jealous anglers have bad thoughts
and plot to harm this bird, who dives
to eat what they would kill for sport.

It's always a mistake to put numbers to your ducklings;
so many of these mickles fail to make it to a muckling.
When their mum swims by with a feathery flotilla
of little bobbing humbugs, remember that there's still a
long career ahead of them as canapés and finger food
for herons, crows and foxes, or whoever may be in the mood.
Could you swear that you saw something where the pike just made a wave?
Don't dwell too much upon it, now; a duckling simply won't be saved.

So white a bird, the egret sails
serene above the Severn mud
that smirches us, but can't assail
so white a bird. We flounder, flail.
We'd rise and follow, if we could,
so white a bird. The egret sails
serene above the Severn mud.

Recalling dull grey flocks that melted in the murk
of muddy stubble fields round Hilperton,
I looked again, still doubtful that these birds at work,
low lit by midday's sunbeams in the thorns,
were fieldfares; as sharply dressed as jays
but monochrome; black checks and greys
to suit the sparseness of the trees;
a jaunty bouncing on the breeze
then bobbing down and gulping haws in time
to the tolling of an unheard chime
that marked the passing winter's day.

If I were an egg, which thank goodness I ain't,
a guillemot's egg I would be
with an end that's round and the other that's a point
for to stop me from rolling in the sea, the sea, the sea
for to stop me from rolling in the sea.

Heron

You're never really confident
it's not a garden ornament
so silently it stands, intent
on what may be below;

but get too close, it breaks its stare
abruptly, and with greatest care
unfolds itself into the air
and leaves, aloof and slow.

The ibis walks on legs so stiff
it looks like its own hieroglyph
in ancient Egypt, where it struts
so nobly on the walls at Luxor.
Don't bother searching on the Nile;
it's not been seen there for a while,
since the marshes where it hid
were drained and sprayed with pesticid.
Nil desperandum, though, just yet –
we get them now in Somerset!

Jay

Bluff Squire Western, Humphry Clinker,
comic, bucolic, a bit of a stinker,
shouty, squawky, ventriloqual,
moustache twirly, mad as Torquil,
acorn questing Don Quixote
planter of a thousand oak trees
saunters in a hopping way
panached
bright feathered
popinjay

The well-heeled red kites of both Berkshire and Bucks
have gone up in the world, and wherever you look
they are wheeling and whistling with insouciance,
their eyes on the suburbs, their minds on the chance
of chorizo or pâté de lapin sauvage;
although if the locals aren't giving it large
and their bird tables simply have nothing to tarry on
they'll wheel away, whistling, and keep calm and carrion.

elbowed by that north wind
I step aside and see it
fling the lark skyward

black and white shuttlecock
tangled in the trees
magpie, magpie
bouncing on the breeze

There's something about the nightingale's song
that makes folk determined to play along;
like Beatrice Harrison's cello on the BBC
and those RAF bombers on their way to Germany;
or that piano orchestration by Olivier Messiaen
which was musically impressive but a rotten impressiaen.
Still, good, bad or indifferent, they all fail
to make any difference to the nightingale
who sings for ears that aren't human at all;
if there's no-one in the forest where its song falls
does it make a sound? Oh, bless;
the answer to that's an enormous yes.

Below Butland Wood I stop to watch
the barn owl beat its slow silence, valley long,
ghost white against the beeches.

Dropping now to the farm tucked up in dusk
I hear those small unnoticed sounds return;
the hill's herd, the sea beyond,
slow breath, that pulse in my ear.

If you would view the ptarmigan
pton your thickest cardigan
to keep you warm, before you stroll
up to those peaks that they ptrol

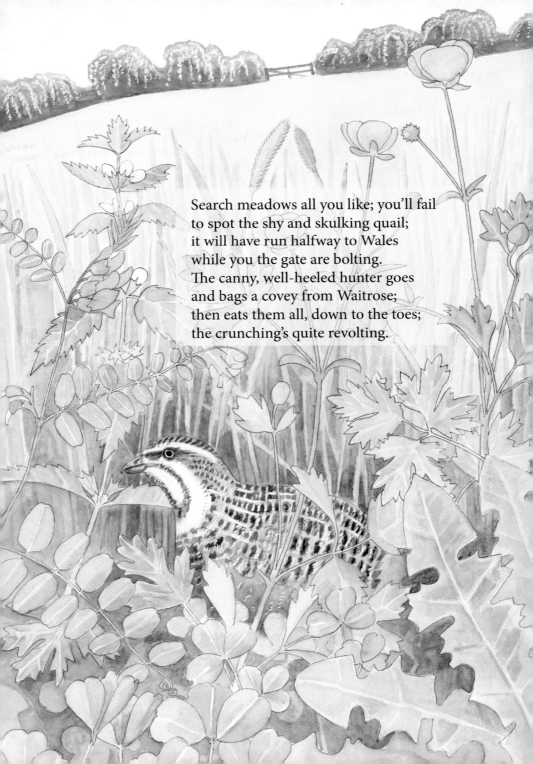

Search meadows all you like; you'll fail
to spot the shy and skulking quail;
it will have run halfway to Wales
while you the gate are bolting.
The canny, well-heeled hunter goes
and bags a covey from Waitrose;
then eats them all, down to the toes;
the crunching's quite revolting.

Partrishow Raven

Sweetest of winds is the summer's, blown from Llanbedr Ystradwy,
tanged by sheep tallow, plumped with bracken, whinberry.
Sweeter, that, than week-dead lamb, bramble-bound; soft as eyes.
I spread wings' fingers, feel the lift and ride the rise,
the heft of sun hot air, fling my cronk to Euas' answering crags.

Fine, too, though, the winter gale, fling of sleet spindrift on Crug Mawr;
a culling cold, with sudden gluts; spilled guts of hare at the field's corner,
blood on the snow. I wipe my beak and throw myself aloft,
tumble on sky's torrent, tuck my wings and fall;
flick, bounce high, and laugh at such wild airness of it all.

Sparrowhawk

Your doubt defines it   its last meal
had no idea that it was there
an arrow flash   the woods now still
a hawk sized absence in the air

Mistle Thrush and Song Thrush

The skirlock, the felfit, the stormcock and thrush
sings in the spring from the top of the bush
while the throggle and thirstle, the mavis and dirsh
is eating a snail (after bashing it first)

Praise now the slighted urban pigeon
its top end coo, its bottom stygian
with mens sana in corpore sano
it rides aloft on heaps of guano

With all bags packed and ready for the off,
I took my final coffee out into the yard,
sounded out the night. The frost was hard,
the air sharp in my nose. It was that lost

quiet time between midnight and dawn.
The houses were asleep. High up, a skein of geese
went ghosting through the stars, passed by Orion,
and flew on south in silence, or at least

if they did call to each other, they were far too high
for me to hear. Maybe they dozed a little as they flew.
Maybe, like me, that night they also knew
that strange sad joy of travelling under such a sky

Sedge Warbler

It churrs and fizzes on for hours; it's funny,
longer than the Duracell bunny's
its damn song. Far off, the slow cuckoo
sings one short note
and then sings two

XXXXing*

The woods are never peaceful in the spring;
the clattering rooks are cawing fit to bust,
and every bird that can do starts to sing.

To tell one song from t'other, that's the thing;
the blackbird, chaffinch, blackcap, wren and thrush;
the woods are never peaceful in the spring.

Sweet though the sound is to our ears, the sting
is that there's really nothing more than lust
and lebensraum behind the stuff cocks sing;

they'd go for almost anything with wings;
if female, chatted up; if male, then cussed;
the woods are far from peaceful in the spring.

Folk too (or so I've heard) will have their fling,
for all too soon we all must come to dust.
Time then enough to rest; it's spring!
Bring in the May; let all things living sing!

singing, of course

Yellowhammer

The eggs of the yoldring are spotted and squiggled
and look like they may have been written by hand;
the resemblance to writing is one that has niggled
such people as fear what they don't understand

and, believing it must be the work of the devil
they'd smash them, and kill the poor bird if they could.
How lucky that these days there's no-one who revels
in daftness like this, and we're all wise and good.

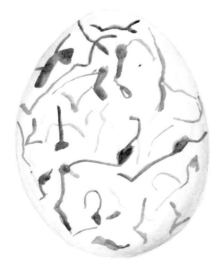

Widewater

"He tried to get the moorings there removed" said Julian off Bimble –
Julian cuts grass for Wiltshire Council, shifts the roadkill –
"mostly you can chuck it through the hedge, but cats and dogs
get taken in, whatever state they're in, and logged;
someone might be missing them." He sails the pounds
from Hungerford to Horton, more or less, stays round
the Vale of Pewsey where he works. We met at dawn.
A kingfisher bashed a minnow on the branch, then darted on,
a quick blue spark against Widewater's reeds.
"Spent thousands on the legal fees, for all the good it did.
Still, he keeps the gate locked at the top of the track;
can't keep folk out, there's been a path since back
before King Alfred came and met his thanes,
there on the tump. They went and beat the Danes,
way up there on the Downs. See the lane?
The winter the canal froze hard,
they had to carry coal and water down from the end."

A buzzard circled Pickle Hill; the stockman on his quad
moved the electric fence across the field a little way,
called out in Polish for the herd to graze.
We brushed the dew off meadowsweet
and butterbur, grown shoulder high,
through which the ways to moorings had been bashed
for boats at least half hidden from the track;
 Eve, Netty, Bimble, Jessie, Arran; making home
here for a few more days, then moving on.

Below the big ash, where the ground is clear,
around last night's fire circle lay empty cans of beer
and smoke-blacked cooking pots on half a scaffold plank.
A small child's bicycle leaned on the bank.
Across the bridge we passed the big new house
in whose walled gravel courtyard sat a Jag.
Along the drive's wide closely-tended verge,
rebellious moles had tumped the smooth mown grass,
and grey hairs on a strand of wire showed how
the badger made its customary way
into the pasture where, above the grazing Jacob flock,
the tilting billboard claimed 'we want our country back'.

It's a tricky business thinking of birds for some letters, especially towards the end of the alphabet where they seem to have shovelled in all the odd ones. So I didn't really try too hard with Z, although the poem *does* contain a buzzard. Still, to show willing...

This zebra finch
would cheerfully lynch
anyone who put another bird instead
for the letter z